YOUNIVERSE

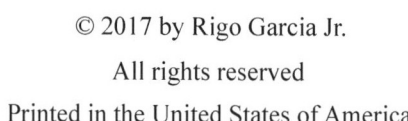

© 2017 by Rigo Garcia Jr.
All rights reserved
Printed in the United States of America

This book or any portion thereof
may not be reproduced or used in any manner whatsoever
without the express written permission of the publisher
except for the use of brief quotations in a book review.

5.06" x 7.81" (12.852 x 19.837 cm)
Black & White on White paper
210 pages
Rigo Garcia Jr.
ISBN-13: 978-0692906705 (Custom Universal)
ISBN-10: 0692906703 (Createspace)
BISAC: Poetry / American / General
First Printing, 2017

www.rigogarseajr.com

YOUNIVERSE

BY GARSEA

for you,

from the universe

The Foreword

Today is Friday, July 28th 2017 9:34 p.m.

i am twenty-two years old but after reading what i've written in this book i feel like an old man on his death bed who carefully translated his strange mind his old soul and his ambiguously afflicted life into two-hundred and ten pages of vulnerability for you to parallel intersect and/or diverge with.

introspectively i don't feel my body's age regardless of what it tells me. i've had a varying degreed experience with love tragedy loss bliss mayhem and fear that has consistently altered my perspective and continuously expanded my *what seems like* boundless growth and understanding.

when i was growing up i always felt estranged from those around me. i moved around a lot in my youth and had to leave materialism and people i cared about behind without a choice. though i never packed much my traumas always made sure they remained part of my baggage. interestingly enough i became immensely socially and environmentally adaptable and developed an acute ability to make meaningful connections quickly and effortlessly with strangers.

but uprooting a lot had its cruel repercussions. i unconsciously developed a rolling stone complex that would affect my life indefinitely. the more homes and loved ones i left the more i became distant from others and myself. my roots ceased to go deep into my environment. i grew troubled and internally conflicted with the ills of my harsh reality. my roots were severed and i lost connection with the most important person i could lose touch with, *myself.*

from my childhood through my teens i had a lack of guidance and an abundance of misguidance with little to no community support in a broken home built on instability.

i was raised in poverty with a middle-class-life illusion by polar opposite parents; a young single mother who sacrificed her youth for my well-being and an incarceration-prone alcoholic felon of a father whose charm and intellect became his detrimental demise. fortunately, i had the opportunity my parents never had but conflictingly their issues and their parent's issues and their parents parent's issues were projected and passed on to me inter-streamed with the blood in my veins.

being that i was fourth generation mexican-american my culture and roots were lost from most of my experience. neither of my parents spoke spanish fluently so my tongue didn't speak a lick. my passed down name was the only remains of my egotistical father and an unfamiliar culture i was supposedly rooted from.

simply put, *i was americanized.*

but through deculturalization i've come to realize that i inherited problematic ideals and self-sabotaging coping mechanisms and i was generationally conflicted. it has taken my lifetime to get to where i am now. though i'm mentally equivocal i have found enough internal resolution to be able to find external solutions to problems that have impaired generations before me, the resolve is beautiful unique and tangible and now in *your* hands.

i came to write this book inspired by many things but *milk & honey* by rupi kaur and Tupac Shakur's *A Rose that Grew from Concrete* were by far the biggest inspirations.

A Rose that Grew from Concrete was the book that introduced me to poetry. i could relate to Tupac's struggle in ways i wasn't able to relate to someone. he seemed to effortlessly understand me through his emotionally raw writing, this made me not feel alone in my thoughts and emotions, it inspired me to write.

milk & honey was a different kind of inspiration.
i felt rupi's pain, society's inflicted oppression on her life, the unwritten narrative, the power of simplicity. it was an immensely intimate experience. while reading her writing it felt like i was talking with a friend i knew for a lifetime. the words danced on the pages and the abstract drawings allowed me to share her mind and let our hurt connect and heal. i had never experienced something in the written language like that, i was once again inspired.

but this time, not just to write but to create a similar experience of self-expression that goes beyond self-therapy and into collective connection and healing. i felt inclined to do this.

i began to take my own writings out of the shackles of my mind and the dungeons of my traumas. i started unhinging the bolts of every cell-door and examining what was within each of them in hope to be brave enough to bring them into the light to meet the sun,
your eyes.

when the eighteen year old me started writing it was solely to express the hurt out of me not to revisit it. but the more time i spent with hurt and words the more i fell in love with the beauty of them.

i discovered that the ability to express myself was internally gratifying and therapeutic. i didn't think there was anything more i could get out of writing. but then i found something beyond my ego, i found that the ability to share and connect with another human-being was and is fulfilling beyond the realm of self-gratification.

i learned that craving connectivity comes naturally to all of us but being able to actually connect can be troublesome. i believe that writing has given me the tools to build a bridge to connect with the disconnected, the lost, and the like-minded.

i hope my writing connects with you and does what others have done for me, which is, inspire to create, to grow, to love without condition and to not allow the cruelty of the world to outlast the kindness of it.

this is my hurt, my joy, my loves, my life, my truth.
it's here for *you* to leaf through like making your way through the amazon rainforest without a blade, to feel like the blind to braille, to relate to like the painter to the writer, to connect to like the puzzle pieces on the kitchen table in a cozy home, it's me in the rawest of forms.

—*Rigo Garsea Jr.*

P.S.

as you've already noticed the writing style here is very unorthodox.
i adapted this style from rupi kaur and for some of this book i used it.
the main reason is the simplicity and the other is preference.

for a long time i was so concerned with the structure the punctuation and
every grammatical mishap of my writing that i lost raw self-expression and
found walking on eggshells writing. writing became frustrating.

i've realized that perfectionism and writing are like trying to mix water and
oil. there is and will never be a final draft, only a draft you're okay with
others seeing, judging, and feeling.

my main concern is making sure my words carry the feelings i felt when i
wrote them. you'll see my style in writing change throughout the book to
try to achieve this. *i did the best i could.*

CONTENTS

güero..3

bones made of glass...55

i i i..83

my naked mind..113

scars are my tattoos...153

güero

Love & Fear

are my

Death & Taxes

the universe left us love
our bones are made of stars
we don't find ourselves
we create ourselves
and *that* is who we are

the sun is in our eyes
the moon is in our hearts
the joy is in our souls
the pain is in our art

—*cosmic dust*

i came into this world crying.

i hope to go out smiling.

—*self-eulogy*

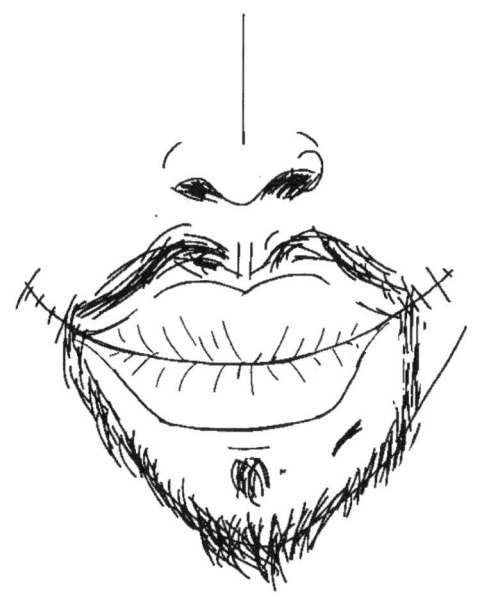

to share silence with you
is intimacy,
your depth is a god complex
of intricacy.

your face
lights up like sage
in a depression filled space,
you're handcrafted
but broken
like cracks in a priceless vase.

you were not created
to attain this world's perfection,
you were made to be a compass
to those with no direction.

—imperfectly perfect

i have never met a soul like yours
she said sadly
have you never looked in a mirror
i replied

—*soul mirror*

my body craved as many women as possible
a high body count is praised
society told me that
this was okay.
i was even told that women were inferior
that love wasn't real and there's always an ulterior
motive that i'll miss
but i got to thinking for me this won't exist.
because my mother taught me differently
my mother was strong, fearsome,
she showcased resiliency.
she wasn't a piece of meat,
not some *thing* you find in the gutter of your street
definitely not expendable
so i ask
may my mind be mendable
from this broken rape culture;
may it be shaped like Michelangelo's most famous sculpture
may it stay in the sky and not on the ground with the vultures.
may it be bright as the sun and not dull and dim
may it not be like my father who was the coward,
the absent, the alcoholic, the grim
i don't know why
i ever idolized him...

—false idols

you're an animal

she moaned while we were on the floor of her room 12:25AM

that felt so good

she whispered as she turned her back to me to sleep 12:40AM

that was it

i thought questionably as my fourteen year old heart found its rhythm 1:00AM

i feel empty

was the last thought i had before i got up and walked out the bedroom from her twenty-three year old body 4:25AM

—*my first time*

how could you use my body
with such ease
you stole the rest of my youth
away from me
it was all i had
you gutted me
you physical touched me
but never loved me

—my eyes are abandoned aqueducts

you speak in every language
know every fingerprint by name
you even show the blind
that we all see the same.
you have lived forever
withstood the ills of time
been there in the open
or a companion confined.
i can find you everywhere
the trees
the street
the metallic or plastic
the concrete
making symphonies
even in the walking
cadence of my feet.
you can be quiet
or loud and fill a room
connect millions
or make a flower bloom
you are
music.

—*the universal language*

not until i lost what i loved
did i become afraid
not until someone left me
did i never stay
not until i lost care
did i find hate
not until i found destiny
did i discover fate

—*the contrast*

for the first time
in a long time
i felt comfortable like your favorite pair of shoes
i felt warmth like a campfire in mid june
i felt connected as the birds to the sky
i felt so happy i'd be content if i died
you held me
i felt home in you
i was falling asleep
i wanted to tell you *sweetdreams Celeste*
but for reasons unknown
my mind thought to say your name
and hers slipped out

—*regret*

i told you
i don't love you.
what i really meant was
i don't know how to love you.

—*a mistake*

everyone is staring,
how did the invisible man become the center of attention?
the room is growing smaller
we're packed in like sardines
my heart-beat is doing jazz improvisation time signatures
my clothes turn to boa constrictors
i feel my forehead leak sweat
i'm having a heart attack
i feel nauseous
i hurry outside
but not before
someone grabs a needle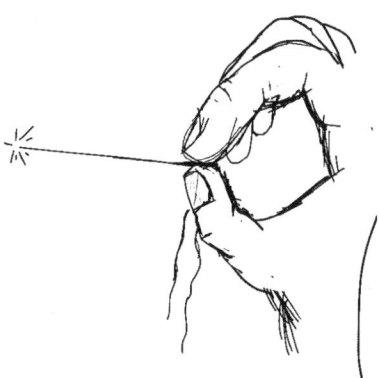
and slips it
between my ribs
my lungs are deflating
i can't breath

—*my first anxiety attack*

i didn't want to have sex
all i wanted was for you to hold me.
you went out drinking with your coworkers
so i said *you can come over but you can't bring anyone.*
you came but not alone
you brought your intentions.
i felt pressured
because usually the woman wouldn't want to have sex
not the man.
the man should always want to have sex
right ?
so i tried for you
but midway through i had to stop.
i felt like someone grabbed the belt
from my pants on the floor
and put it around my neck.
i stopped
you were worried
i laid by the open window
while you rubbed my back
i got quiet
i wanted you to leave
you didn't understand
and neither did i.

—i never learned to say no

i can make the quiet talk until their jaws break from the
heaviness of the amount of words they want to say.
i can make the loud close their mouth as if it was sewn shut
and make them open their ears like a woman spreads her legs
when she wants a man to bear her child.
i can turn ugliness into beauty.
i can alter personalities.
i can make any possibility
a high probability.
i can change fire into water
and anchors into balloons
but for whatever reason
i cannot seem to change
you

—*dead weight*

they're in full effect
always when you're gone
one is always on your shoulder
it's frozen flutter is forever bronzed

you're winter solstice sunkissed
by god the universe the divine
they're your jesus symbol
and they're my alchemist sign

be it by design
i see them everywhere
be it by the times
their migration fills the air

　—the monarch butterfly

what's your definition of love you asked
jessie i said softly hoping you wouldn't hear.
anger and sadness filled your eyes.
i tried to explain
but all you heard was
i don't love you like i love her.

—*she was love*

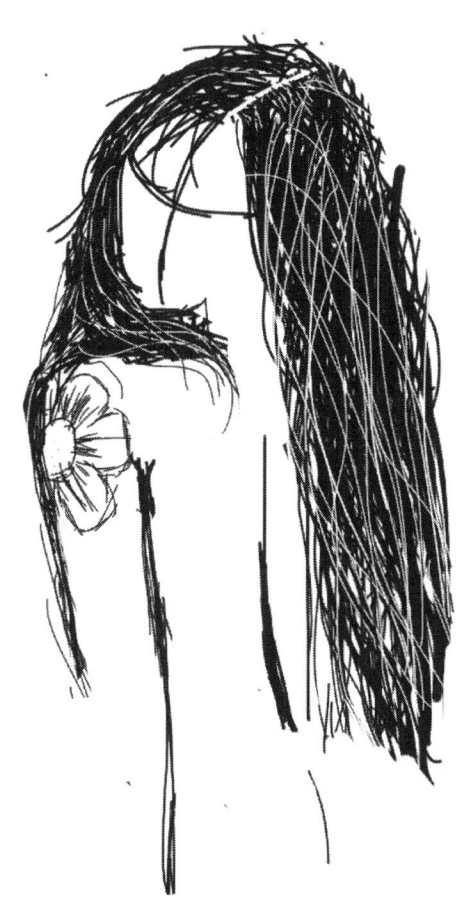

when things are too good to be true
they probably are.
it should strike worry or doubt
or fear in me but it doesn't.
with you i don't seem to care.
you want me to disagree
you want conflict
you want me to be emotional
but i can't.
i just want to love you
give you what you want
give you what you need
give when i have nothing
give when *i* need
because i don't matter
and that's what love is
or at least what it needs to be right now

—numb

she sucked my future
i licked her past
we met in the present
a timeline crash

—*in lust with yo*u

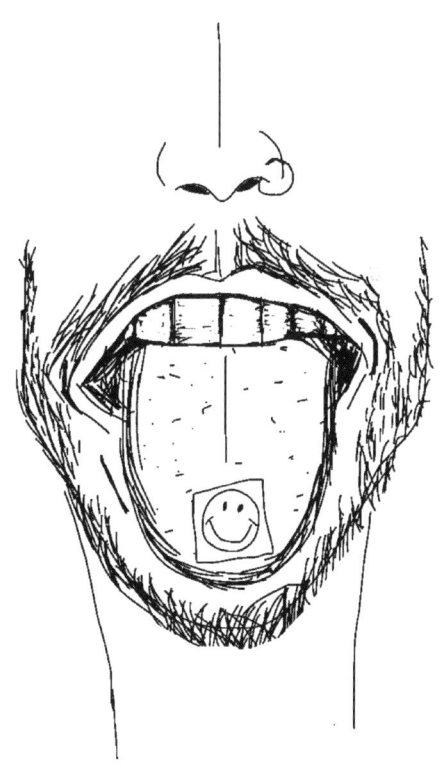

i looked in the mirror and seen a blemish
i picked at my face and noticed another layer

i pricked
then noticed my face was like a thick layer of old wallpapers

i peeled
one for every year every lover every loss every shred of every memory

i tore
until my fingernails broke

i tore more
until every color and pattern was gone

i was torn
and left with
an empty room full of bloody fingernail carvings on blushing pale white walls

—*my face*

it's not why you say it
or how you say it
but when you say it

—timing

i looked into those
familiar brown eyes
she waited
and waited
until the last drop of love
fell from her hopeful words
i love you. . .

there was silence.

she broke it with a sad *sigh*
as if preparing herself.
her intuition must have known.

do you still love me? she asked

an insecure reflex
fell from my mouth's
cold anticipated reply
then
doubt filled my irises
and ice my veins
i uttered
i don't love you
and i never did.

—*the heart i always broke*

i had no idea

i could cause a natural disaster

until i seen the aftermath of her life without me

—*hurt knows her*

i didn't want him to touch me
but i started to fall asleep
we were in the attic
his wife and newborn
were downstairs out of reach
he was massaging me
my head to my feet
in any other case
this wouldn't be okay
but he was a youth pastor
and i was a lost cause

—when i tried to find god

i laid on the sidewalk because i couldn't get up
the concrete must have wanted to hold me
my stomach heaved
i laid in small pools of vomit
Are you okay? Do you need a ride somewhere?
an angel called from inside her car
i could barely walk see or think
i got up
got into the stranger's car
i'm sorry
i told her repeatedly
it's my birthday
i tried to justify

—*my first blackout at twelve years old*

i laid on your couch
waiting for you to come back inside
i brushed my teeth so they wouldn't smell like E&J
i laid and waited
until you finally came
you let me lay in your lap
you rubbed your gentle hands
over my buzzed cut hair
and across my youthful face
you held me
and in the first time in a long time i didn't feel numb
i felt something unfamiliar
the feeling slowly seeped from my eyes

i cried
which i hadn't done in years
no one had caressed me like that since my mother
i cried and watched puddles turn into streams
to rivers to oceans to swollen grey clouds of rain
i could have flooded the world with that amount of salt water.
i finally felt like everything would be okay
but then
you told all my cousins that i cried
i remember the bruises the bullying the mental torment

—because boys don't cry

HELP ME !
HELP ME !
HELP !
i screamed as i clamored the fiber glass back door with the side of my fist with the force of a judge's gavel.
i wake up startled
i'm in the neighbors backyard
Why am i banging on their back door? i thought
the neighbor is staring at me concerned and confused
i'm barefoot, my feet are dirty, i walk through their house out the front door and back to my house without speaking a word
i put clothes by my door to create some type of false security
i lock the door
i'm scared
What's wrong with me? i thought as i cried myself to sleep

—when my sleepwalking got bad

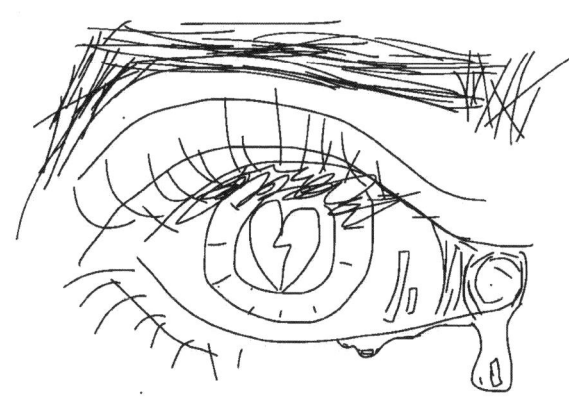

i stare at you.
*i've never woke up by a lover
especially someone so beautiful.*

*it must be your energy
or maybe it's the calm cadence in your breathing.*

i wonder if you're dreaming.

one hair is slightly in your face.

i watch you sleep
i lay on your chest
to listen to your heartbeat.

then i get up
kiss your cheek
and do what i do best
leave.

—a first time that doesn't hurt

you spoke of angels
i listened in awe
you knew God
on a personal level
you spoke in tongues with no flaws.
what a godly man i thought of you
i found what a holy man looked like
it was *you.*
but later i would find something different
something dark and something hidden
a shameful secret.
you touched your daughters
in places that were sacred and not for your hands
they would bury the trauma in their memory-cemetery
only to ever be dug up by men like you
you disgusting sick monster

—they call you my grandfather

my dad died and i was never told why.
i have attachment and trust issues.
i never learned self-love.
i get depressed often.
i don't feel like a man but i'm called one.
my childhood wasn't easy but i continuously minimize it.
i'm searching for a purpose that i don't think i'll ever find.
i can't find or create a meaning for my life.

i have blind faith with love.
people take advantage of me.
i believe in the potential of people.
i can't say no.
my bestfriend doesn't know what to do when i'm depressed.
i isolate myself when i just want someone to hold me.
i think the world is dying.
i have a hard time crying.

i feel like a coward.
somebody molested some of my sisters.
my dad would beat my mom.
my favorite jeans are ripped.
it feels like everyday I re-live my traumas.
i recirculate bad memories.
i can't block out the thoughts.
some mornings i wish i didn't wake up.

—*raw & unfiltered*

i found a rose that grew from concrete
it laid severed and trampled
i picked it up
not to keep
but to find it a home

—*you*

my bloodline is
the colonizer and the colonized
so who am i ?

my blood's native tongue
is foreign to me
my accent is hidden
unfortunately
generations assimilated
racially affiliated
my skin color
was never discriminated
i was somehow fortunate
emancipated
because the lighter the skin
the falsely liberated
and the easier the life

—they call me Güero

he burned me in three places
two on my right forearm and one of my belly
every once in awhile
i stare at them
to see if *it* really happened

—*a troubled child*

you live your life
thinking that you know what will happen next
then you fall in love or lose someone
and everything changes

—*love*

you're my morning coffee
she said through her gentle smile
while she held her favourite mug by her lips

—the morning of

there are some who will make you forget
others will make you remember
some will make you whole
others will dismember
you. . .
—

i don't know how to love
i told her embarrassed
be gentle
she whispered in my ear

—*making love*

you don't know how ugly you are
until you meet someone beautiful

you begin to hate yourself
when you don't change your ways

misery seeps from your thoughts
to your words to your actions

then you look in the mirror
and break it

—*broken*

i dreamt i was drowning.
they looked down at me with blank stares
i had no control of my life
i had no father
no mother
no guidance,
my kind loving innocence
found violence.

—*on my own*

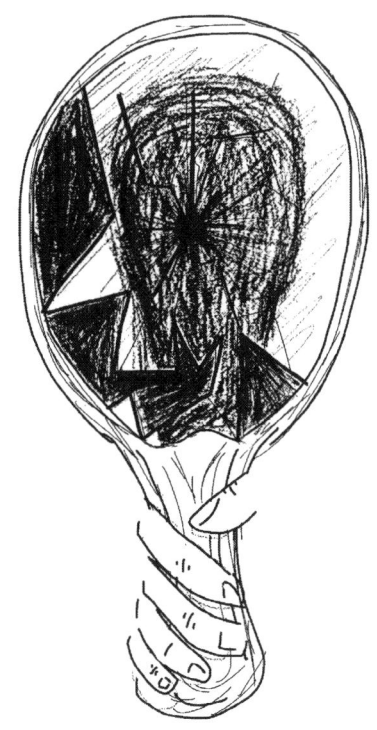

but you don't know what dying feels like
she said dismayed
i don't know what living feels like either
i replied
then hung up the phone

—*melodrama*

as a kid you are taught
you can be whoever you want
then you grow up and realize that's a lie.
you are then unconsciously demanded
to be who everyone else wants you to be
then you realize you can't make everyone happy.
then you really grow
you then realize that the kid in you was right all along.

—*circles*

being fully vulnerable
allowing myself to hit rock bottom
after falling in love
has been the bedrock of my growth.

only in desolation
have i rediscovered myself
i drowned
i learned to float.

loving another
without fear
has taught me courage
and foolishness.

but giving someone
my heart to break,
to stab, to trample
has taught me selfishness.

showing someone my scars
was like giving them
the missing piece of the puzzle.

—regret

who are you she asked
i delicately touched her face and said
i am everything you ever wanted
but will never allow yourself to have

—*forgive yourself*

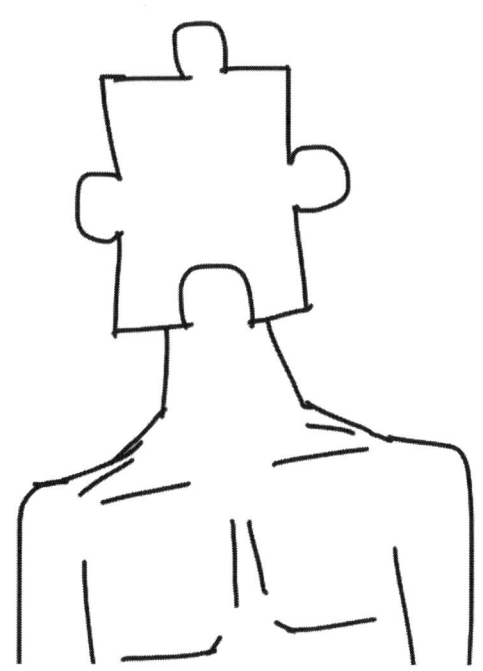

June 22nd 2016

you laid on the hospital bed
swollen from all the medicine they injected in you
tubes were down your throat
a machine was keeping you alive

i knew you weren't there anymore
your body felt empty when i walked in the room
the doctor's asked what i wanted to do
i had three choices
but they all ended with you dying
it was only a matter of *when*

family members came and cried on you
when i was alone with you
i cried on you too
i said my goodbye
but it felt empty inside

i told them *the one with no pain*
the doctors nodded in agreeance
they gave me one of your only possessions, a ring
and the rest of the memory is a blur

—i pulled the plug

i have become
uncomfortable with my presence
is this why i don't like to be lonely ?

—*a question*

i can't be how i am with him like i am with you she said

he'll never be me and i'll never be him i replied

she nodded as if she already knew

i told her *the people you love are like flowers in a garden. each is different and has its own place it can grow. make sure you're trying to give him his own place.*

i got out the car
and she drove away

—the parking lot

i am sensitive

i tried to fight against myself and not be
but i am
one word can change my entire day
for better and for worse

—delicate

others have made the common mistake
of thinking they know where i have been
because of how i dress
how i carry myself
how i talk
the words i use.
don't make that mistake
you don't know
where these feet full of scars have been
and i don't know where yours have been

—lets get to know each other

bones made of glass

You've made it through
the road of thorns
you're purpose set
passion sworn

You'll be adored
but first ignored
they'll never see
who you're for

It'll be too late
so rest your eyes
smell the roses
don't you cry

Smile, and let it be
find your roots and grow like trees
be the sequoias
move with the breeze

You are the sun & the moon in one
god's debris and the sweetest rum
the wind child without care
the rising and setting sun
the last lunar flare

—child of the wind

You want poetry?
How about the blood of my pen?
You want mountains?
How about the mustard seeds planted in my brain
whose roots have disguised themselves as my veins?
I can move mountains.

You want heartbreak?
I can give that to you.
I know you can't function without it.
You need some reason to be hurt.
You need someone else to define your worth.

I'm perfect for you.
Can't you tell?

My skin is earthy and I smell of redwoods & cedar
My eyes are worldly and I see only in shades of grey
My hands are worthy only for your endless oceans
My heart beats for you but skips from fear of reposition

I'm perfect for you.

I am the whisper of your name
I am the lover who will always break your heart
I am the disappearing footprints behind you on the beach
I am your shadows only friend
I am the dark.

At night I will consume you,
light can no longer keep you from me
I am the thoughts you keep to yourself
I am the screams you recite to yourself
I am your reflection.

A broken mirror
or a ripple in the water will never separate us
A fragment or a water's echo could never betray us
I am with you in your sleep and when you wake up
I am you.

I wish I could accept the love I think I deserve,
the love I know I deserve
like it said it in the book you gave me.

I wish I could talk about love & passion
without sounding crazy.

I wish I could trade the yearnings & cravings
for faith and spiritual saving
I wish I didn't only want you,
to save me. . .

I wish, a kiss, could grip more than a physical vibration
I wish, the lips, could speak more than temptation
but the body lies,
which is why,
when I cry
I wipe my eyes,
the body lies,
my body lies
all alone.

You may have slit your wrist
you may have tried to carve your heart out
You may have felt release
you may have found your art out
but i

I

I've killed myself many times
in ways you can't imagine
I've thought of death every second
time is an illusive fraction

My mind is the real murderer
but they'll blame my hands
My body is the real victim
that eyes
could not understand

The truth is
you don't know me
and you never will

—unknown

I hope you forget how our souls met.

I hope you forget my fingertips that ran through your hair

down your spine

over the goosebumps on your honeyed skin and rugged scars and back around.

I hope you forget the tears I wiped and only remember them falling to your cold pillowcase.

I hope you forgot the feeling of falling

especially in love,

especially with me.

I hope you forget my laugh

and the hurt that comes with it.

I hope you forget the kind words

and only remember the painful ones.

I hope you give another the chance

I could never take.

I hope he holds you when your lips quiver
when you get your anxiety shakes.

I hope you forget my scent when I'm with her.

I hope you forget how our bodies align and your memory withers.

I hope you forget my comforting sweet words

and it becomes as if you've never heard them

or they become flat and bitter. . .

Her tongue was sharp as razorblades
her skin soft as silk,
her love was sweet as honey
and soothing as a cup of warm milk.

—*My Milk & Honey*

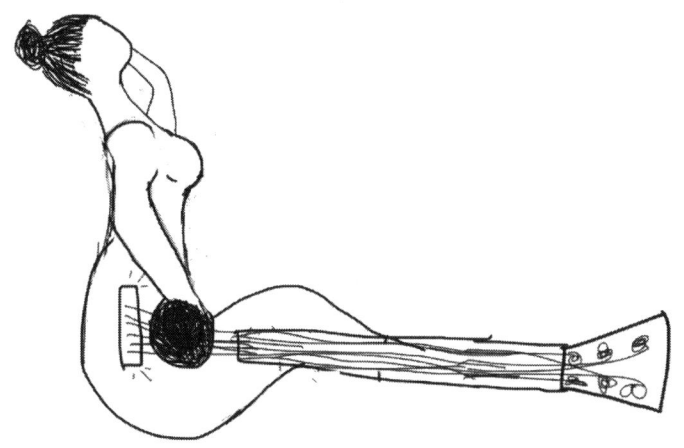

You're my ice cold glass of water on a hot summer's day.
You're the hot tea in my favorite cup in mid winter haze.
You're the map to the unsolvable maze.
You are, the book i don't want to ends last page.

You're the relief after a pregnancy scare.
You're my post-anxiety attack's breath of fresh air.
Please don't say you don't care
we both know
that's all you ever do.

—be yourself

I walk out the back door and join you on the steps
you turn to me and I could smell your alcoholic breath.
I look into your eyes and I see the regret,
you say, "be better than me, don't be like the rest"

I stare and want to speak
my words and thoughts become bare
so I stare, I stare
i *stare* into eyes desperate for repair.

I gather up the courage and try to speak
but depression and regression hold my tongue.

You look at me and exert a tired sigh,

"You're my son and I love you so
I want you to know something before I go.
These chains have held me, my entire life
generations before me its time for you to make it right."

You pull me close and tears follow,
years of fears that left you hollow
I embrace and I know what I need to do
I look into your eyes and say, "I'll be a better you."

—*memories I won't forget*

I'm feeling naked, while our clothes are on
It's been a week so I'm feeling strong…
I never stayed
so now you're gone

mind & body.

You make forever, seem like a day
if it's meant to be, you know what they say
they say let it be, but I don't believe
you'll ever come back, to ever loving me

mind & body.

You make forever, seem like its real
Its cold in this place, my hands I can't feel
if you want to leave then be like the breeze
I have loved you and done it
always with ease

mind & body.

Don't you cry
wipe your eyes
I've always tried
when you never did

—the love that was never mine

I never thought,
I could feel this way again
I don't know how, to ever tell my friends
I feel like they can't understand
how it is, the ocean loves the land.

I've spent so much time, trying to run away
that I couldn't stop and enjoy the day
I know now I, kept it all inside
there you were with love
when my father died.

The horizon loves the rise
the sun loves the moon
the darkness loves the sky
and the summer loves June.
Why ?
did I always push
and tears I only pulled
I thought I seen forever
but I see now that I was fooled.

—*never ready*

You'll want to hate me
but you'll never be able to.
You'll want me to love you
but I'll never be stable enough.

—*Unrequited Love*

we've been through it all
but they'll never know

we've held each other on the floor of your van
in the cold
with only your favorite blanket
and the warmth of our bodies
we've shivered the night away
we've had no homes

we ate together
we slept together
we laughed together
we loved together
we were so good together
until i felt you couldn't get better
until i felt i couldn't get better
i started treating you how i felt inside,
terrible.

i'm sorry i projected
it's my feelings i protected
your heart i infected
with the disease
of a heartbreak

—lonely nights with you

i wouldn't sleep
i couldn't sleep
i'd awake from night terrors
someone's breaking in
i'm paranoid
i don't feel like i can protect you
i'll cower under covers
hide my pride under blankets
reveal my fears in the stillness of night
i'm no man
i'm a boy
who's afraid
who lacked shelter from the storms
the hives will start to swarm
in the form of sweat
bullets
spraying through my pores
there's banging at the door
i gasp
air i cannot breathe
my heartbeat beating out of me
i find composure and
you're sleeping calmly beside me

—the sleepwalker

you allowed me in your home
when i had no where to go
you showed me love
and gave me room to grow.

there's always room for someone in need
there's always one more plate when there's a mouth to feed
my home is your home
my family is your family
it's what you'd tell me.

you'd teach me
like your own son
i'd think
what do you want from me?
i even tried to run.

but it turns out you wanted nothing
you loved me and still do,
like rocks love river water
the one's covered in mildew.
you gave me guidance
you gave me unconditional love
you came in the form of a long awaited friend
you showed me kindness that i thought would have its end
but it didn't and never has
thank you my lifelong friend

—*Orozco*

I found a home for heartbreak.
I've decided I won't leave this place.
You're the cure for my heartache.
You're my grace
and I'm your grave.
Remember that
embed that in your thoughts
until it becomes
a scar on your brain tissue

—your scar tissue

you found me
when i didn't know that i was lost
i could confide in you
when no one else could talk.
you'd listen
you may not have understood
but you'd listen
and that's what i needed.

i could go over anytime
we would listen to your
favorite records.
you'd sing to me
you were so shy
so beautiful
a blessing in disguise.

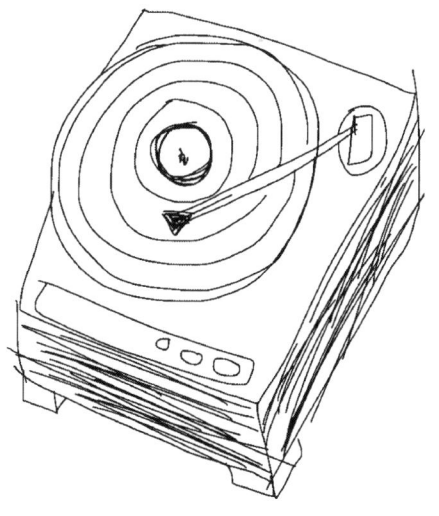

we'd talk for hours
for days
for years
through pain
through versions of me
through layers of me through deep-rooted fears.
you were the bestfriend
i always needed but was always bound to hurt.
i knew this when we first kissed
that death of a friendship we had given birth.

—*ambiguous loss*

You're on the train, stopping by strangers.
Who is to blame ? What is your name ?

You have a baby, close to your chest
you walk aimlessly asking for cents
a dollar at most...

So I wonder—

Where are you going?
Where are you from?
The baby starts crying
and you look so young.

Red is your hair, green in your eyes
beautiful smile but you're crying inside.
"Take my last dollar...
here, I don't need it."
"Thank you sir",
Your eyes have receded.

I feel the shame I feel the guilt
I feel the stares and I feel their filth
Permanent
like the black sharpie on the cardboard cover
sixteen and already a mother...

—the girl on the train

I found a life and people that love me
it rains a lot but is always sunny.
My mind is ugly because I don't want this
being calm, is nostalgic.

If I could leave, I wouldn't go
in my rowboat I'd only float.

I don't ever, seem to stay.
My mother's hair is turning grey.
My dad has passed on, I wish he stayed.
My sisters' need me, but I can't
I can't stay.

If I could leave, I wouldn't go
in my rowboat I'd only float.

Apologies my loves.
Apologies my friends.
Apologies my brothers.
Apologies my sisters.

—my bags are packed

No,
I mean it this time
liquid tears turn to wine.
I've never been yours
and you've never been mine.

—absent self-worth

How do I taste

    when poison is seeping from my pores?

        How does my tongue feel

            when clouded judgment

                starts to pour?

Are you afraid

    of my hands like me?

      I was afraid of his

        I flinched when he'd raise them quickly.

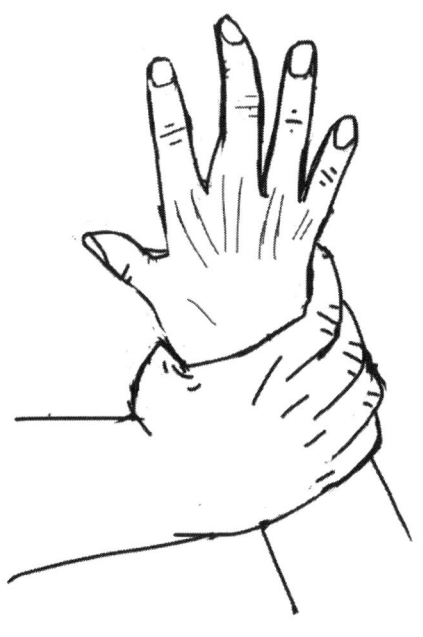

I fear my hands will do the same when you're too close.

I fear that my hands will kill your love and strangle hope.

I fear my hands will grab the silence,
I fear that I will be domestic violence. . .

you wonder why
you sit in your car for hours
you can't understand
how sweet turned sour.

you feel defeat
your favorite songs are on repeat.

you always play your music loud
to drown out the thoughts
but *those* thoughts will find their way through
because eventually your heart will start to skip
along with the CD i made for you.

then you'll hear it
maybe not at first
you'll probably try to ignore it
and avoid the hidden hurt
but the skips will become long eerie screeches
and that's when you'll have no other choice
you'll take the CD out and realize
i'm not around anymore.

—the caravan

you need somebody
but i am nobody
you had my body
and i
couldn't say no...
i could never say no,
never to you.

—I don't get her but I do get hurt

What's going on in my head?
Too many days that I dread.
What's left to be unsaid?
Too much life living half-dead.

Desensitized & conditioned
taught to not lead only listen.
We all live in *a* prison
all religion is factualized fiction.

Man always leads to corruption
corporations promote endless consumption.
Don't jump, to an assumption
because if you take a leap of faith you will not function.

Nine to fives to seven days a week
wired on caffeine, a few hours to sleep.
Processed food that we're taught to eat
global warming has turned up the heat.

Open your eyes and wake up
open your eyes not just to stay up.
Endless bills time to pay up
time to do what you love,
oh wait, the day's up.

—*the paradox of living in America*

Brown eyes,
are brown eyes
until you love someone with brown eyes.

Your eyes
are like a painting
they always seem to say things
like *i love you*
and *i miss you*
and *i'd really like to kiss you*

Brown eyes,
are brown eyes
until you lose someone with brown eyes...

—my favourite iris

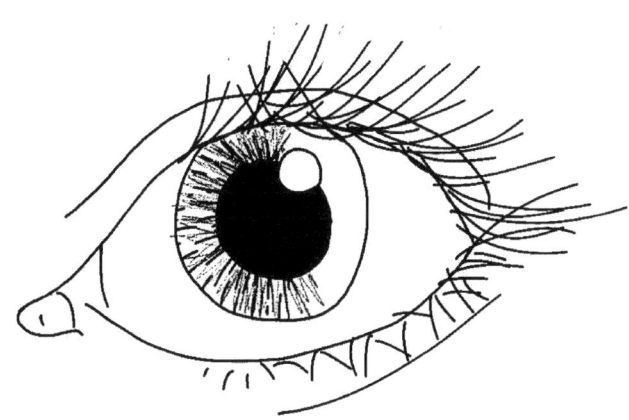

iii

i bought some flowers
only to watch them die.
they need water and sunlight
if i want them to stay alive
but I'm keeping them inside,
with me.

—*The dead flowers on the table*

you're one of a kind
you speak from your heart
but you've cut others
with the fragmented parts
of your broken heart
which stick out like stalagmites

we're two of a kind
we speak the same language
sometimes you feel
i feel your anguish
but truth is i share it
we're soul mates

frequencies align,
you said,
I would describe the world to you
if you ever went blind.

—*unconditional love*

it hurts to write
when my bones feel brittle
when the white walls engulf me and i feel belittled

it hurts
to crave connection
but always be disconnected
they don't understand that
it hurts
not my hands but my brain
all alone
with the blame

it hurts
to want to lay in bed
and not get up
to not exist
no one knows how at risk, i am
not my friends
not a lover
not my mother or brothers
they look
but are unaware
or
they see
and just don't care. . .

—the depressed writer

When it rains
the liquid stains my flesh
the water soaks & sulks
in every misty breath.

The soul knows no weather
only endless extremes
tragedy & catastrophe
seem the common themes.

—i never learned to cope

remember that blame
always needs a home
be it permanent or temporary
blame cannot go
blame is necessary
anger is secondary
to sadness

for blame is the culprit of abuse
that some choose to marry
or wear like their shoes
it's the truth

go ahead you'll learn
internalize it or show it in anger
give it to your loved ones
or shove it on a stranger

blame, needs to be nurtured
for blame is always lost
but when it finds you it's lost no further
the action of the cost

you're home
you hold the shame
but you don't know this
because *your* name is blame

i do not want to believe
that i suffer from depression

—*my worst fear*

you were wise beyond your years
i'm glad i pestered you with questions
your lost soul flooded me with curiosity
and energies of eloquent essence

at times it was difficult
but over time I taught myself patience
falling in love with you was easier than breathing
vernacular vibrations

you're surely not of this earth
you're the epitome of kindness
you did something timeless
you opened my eyelids.

your love, was not of the flesh
your grace in every breath
how do you know these things?
are you an old soul?
every road you must have traveled
every war you must have battled
every mind you must baffle
how?
did you teach me understanding and kindness
how did i master seeing you
even though i was born in blindness?

—*the eyes of the wise*

i love the parts of you
you don't know exist
when you have nothing
look at the scars on your wrists
it's a reminder remember?
when you hid yourself in the restroom
in rainy days November
your hand would start to tremor
when the chemicals began to enter
remember?
the feeling of killing parts of you
feeling the black hole in your brain
your sleeves start to stain
your body will remain
the neurons are still misfiring
death you're romanticizing
it's not what you think
you're seeing hot pink
pulses convulsions
thought repulsion
the mirror repulsive
it wasn't what you wanted

—the tiles on your bathroom floor

i have thought
of writing a suicide letter, to see what i would write.
though i feel guilt with the thought alone
it would be my way of saying *goodbye.*
i have never been good at goodbyes
so i'd like to get this one right.
would you call me a coward for wanting the pain to cease ?
even though i'm at fault chemically ?
i've run out of remedies
is depression how you'd remember me ?

—*a funeral is for the living*

i stopped trying to fill the void
with drugs
with alcohol
with people

i wallow in self-pity
i swallow only poison that i've brewed
i acknowledge that i need to be lonely
only for you

—her name was lonely

Staring, into the earth
caring, cured my worth
baring resemblance to the birth
of the eyes that were hers.

Sadness, tries to pull
dancing demons that are dull
halfway empty halfway full
caressing fiction, I'm a fool.

Now we undress, as we tremble
a sweetness, that is gentle
vulnerable, in my mental
we were, accidental.

Fall in love with you
drive me crazy before I move
sky blue and gentle greens hues
I, am in love with you.

Now we undress, as we tremble
a sweetness, that is gentle
vulnerable, on my mental
we were, incidental.

I realized, I was waiting
scared of someone, not staying
sunshine blue skies and it's raining
earth healer, everchanging.

I don't want to touch your skin,
I don't want to kiss your lips.
I don't want to let you in
my hands are full of sin...

The slither of a serpent's tongue
the feelings of a lover's touch,
the heartbeats the rush
our bones hush.

I'm waiting for sixteen shooting stars
on an overcast night,
when moonlight breaths you
and kisses my sight.

I'm waiting to call your name
footprints on the beach
walk aimlessly
but always out of reach...

—a feeling i will always remember

i always forget
about the birthmark on your neck
until i see you

it's a heart
or a bird depending how you look

to me
it's a symbol
that you speak from your heart
you're an open book
with torn pages
you are mysterious art

—*abstract love*

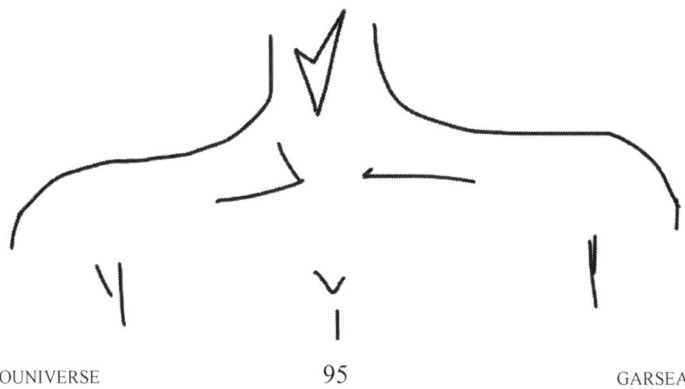

You run like the rivers
run fast and run far.
You run like the rivers
but you can't outrun your heart.

Caged river that wants to be free
rare as you are, you're all that I need
holy and sacred please don't you leave.

Graceful and merciful as lovers touch
powerful and course as waters rush
which have no end
until we meet again.

—my caged river

The first thing I heard was your song
but you said you'd been talking in your sleep
said my fluttering eyelids were ventriloquists
prying meaning from between the sheets.

I see a symphony in your sleeping
you are a song before you wake
but my words are music
and you cannot hear what you will not intake.

—*The world in your eyes*

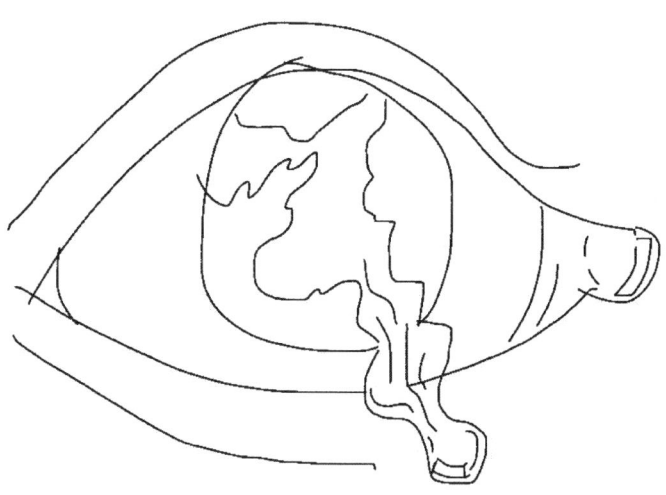

Weak my flesh, alluring angelic
heart of stone, mind on relics.
Burn desires and tainted blood
neck of scars, I have hung.

Strong my mind, desperate demons
silver tongues, gold they're bleeding.
Freezing sleep I'll never awake
all I want is no escape.

Shut me in,
the confines of lunacy
shadows of memories await
take one last look at me.

Ugly to bone, clinging chaos
insecurities, don't take days off.
Suffocate on silence, my severed tongue
all alone, loaded gun.

—*Love is Hate*

WHEN THE SUN LOVED THE RAIN

Everyday I shine for you.
Seasons change but I never do.

I've never known
a love more true,
than what is
between me and you.

Grayness separates us, and I try to break free,
I scour far and wide
so that you can see.
But you never seem to notice,
maybe I'm at fault?
I kiss your remains
on the puddled asphalts...

I wonder,
have you witnessed our beauty?
The flowers we bloom?
Have you seen the destruction,
the gloom the doom
that you've added to?

I've adored and always waited for you,
but you fall for the sky while I fall for you. . .

Misery is sweet
like honey to the bees
like money to our greed
it's nectar we bleed.

Misery is sour
like forgotten melodies
or sullen symphonies
that you'd sing to me.

—the first day of spring

i wonder
if you could love the lonely out of me
i wonder
if i could find honesty
i want you to want me
i'm tired of thinking
i'm tired of drinking
my problems away
i want you to stay
i want to stay
i won't leave this time
i don't make promises
but i promise this time
i promise you
i'll be honest too
don't leave, *please*
i know
i love the wrong parts of you
i'm sorry
i love your body and not your mind
i call you pretty and not beautiful
i say you're amazing and not resilient
i'm sorry
i'm sorry i'm sorry
i'm sorry

—*regret in a bottle*

Empty love always follows
you look strong but you are hollow.

It's been a lifetime of sorrow
tomorrow, seems so far
here you are
sitting in your
broken down car
with a broken down heart.

The broken window
sends cold air
to fill your heaving lungs
and give your goosebumps *goosebumps.*

Clothes and blankets
scattered around and in your trunk
windows are foggy
like your broken glasses
your mirror still works
so fixed smiles you practice.

—bones made of stone

You said i don't look like you
but i have y*our* smile
Your laugh
Your intellect
Your love
Why don't *You* want me?

—*your newborn son*

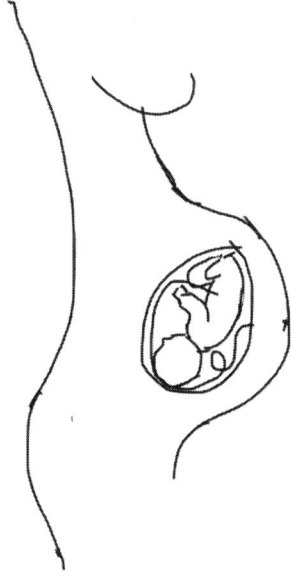

I'm a sober soul with intoxication all around
poison, poison, going down.
A sober soul in a world of affliction
sober soul in a place of addiction.

What's your vice, what's your sin ?
Do you hide away with smoke or gin?
Do you like the needle? Maybe some pills ?
Maybe you like, the withdrawal chills ?

I used to try to kill the anger
with the help of faceless strangers
but I was only killing myself
self-destruction never helps.

Wake up, break down
cold shower
Withdraw, withdraw
cold turkey
Indulge, vomit
whatever can hurt me
No worries
No hurry
Live for the day
and at the end of it plead for God's mercy

—*sober occasions*

Listening to old lovers sing
rusted love on their scratched rings.

I am in a room
they're talking about God
Love & *Realigion* I never thought

—*something to believe in*

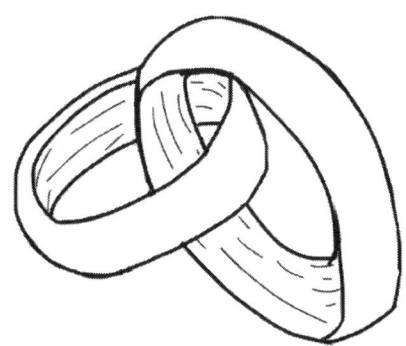

I've been hearing with my eyes
seeing with my ears
been tasting with my hands
and crying in my sleep.

Hiding in an empty room
with the windows covered
can't say bye to any of my friends
not again
moving away, please not again
I can't go back to how I was then.

No mattress, the walls are crying too
lightbulb missing and I'm trying too
I'm trying
to pack my things and stay strong
but I have no control
or at least it's what I tell myself

—The abandoned home

The sun doesn't shine how it used to
I'm alone more than I'm used to
I forgot the passion in my bones,
I lost the life in my roots
I have depression in my eyes,
pale under the black veil
this is what being empathetic entails
a trail of emotions and stagnancy
no compassion, nothing is mattering

—*poverty of mind*

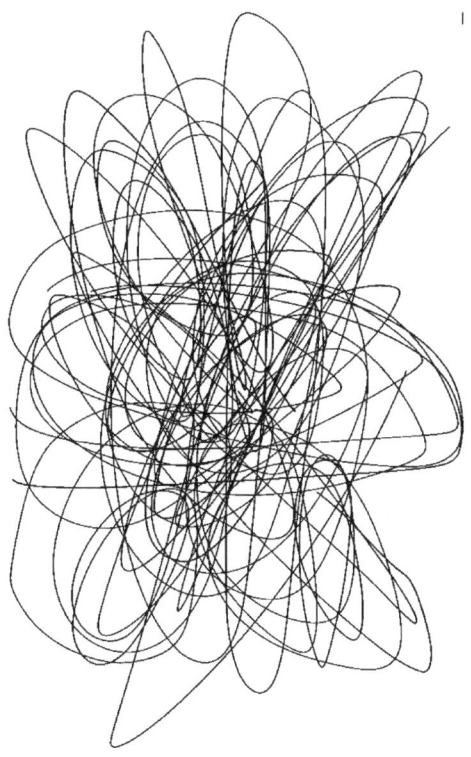

Anxious feelings, biting nails
I have tried and I have failed.
Hopeful days, faces pale
pride that's loud is always frail.

Scratch my skin, till it bleeds
feeling guilt so I do good deeds.
Hide my fears, to conceal
what is fake can seem so real.

I can't seem, to run away
I've tried and tried but always stay.
To feel regret in all my choices
cannot speak silent voices. . .

Ugly truth, halfway lies
halfway house until I die.
Halfway empty, never full
I love you, I'm a fool.

Blinded feelings, biting nails
I have tried and I have failed.
Body braille,
I run my hands
elsewhere now. . .

—body language

my naked mind

Fabricate, the truth before any trace of me is left
'cause if I go, I won't come back, I will never stay.
Litigate, discriminate the after, which I'll attest,
I confess, *I was never happy.*

I've left myself before, broken open doors
there's never been enough but I've always needed more.
Been content, to pretend, I'm okay
defend the ways as I decay
years ago I used to pray.

Ocean skies and cloudy seas, crashing
words with memories, a fairy tale of choice
a lasting voice, everlong the void
no recollection as a boy…

See the Sea proceed to be, everdeep
never need neither you or me
never sleep, days repeat
until we meet, again.

—*Trauma*

Time is confusion, conflicted Confucius.
I can't keep up.

Time is illmatic, to its nasty addicts.
I can't hold on.

Time is strange, it can't be tamed.
I don't have enough.

Time is blame, it's confused my brain.
I need more.

Never too soon but always late
Destiny has had, its time with fate
Time is time for seconds sake.

—a leaf in the wind

I drank and smoked too much
the room is hazy,
feeling down and up
who made me?

Stammer and fall outside
the sky is falling,
fight or flight inside
the street is calling. . .

It's time to end my night
inside I don't feel right
stop and stare
at green street lights

I'm walking to her house
my coat is soaked
rainy nights of doubt
will I sink or float ?. . .

It's time to end my night
inside I don't feel right
stop and stare
at green street lights

—*drunk*

I don't pray before I sleep
Anymore

I don't ask for help
Anymore

I want to lay in bed
close my eyes and stay asleep
Forevermore

I don't want to die
I'm tired on the inside
Forevermore

I want to cut my hair
get my things and leave
Nevermore

The road is my home
look how much I've grown
wish I would have known
Nevermore

—*The traveling soul*

you broke my heart because vulnerability
was always comforting with you,
you've always understood
while you hurt me too.
i blamed you because i was pained
i recited a one sided story i am ashamed.
and even though no relations remain
i hold on, to the ashy remains. . .

The truth can be ugly
and that's the truth,
and truth is *i still love you*

My first love,
i became deranged
love to lust to ambiguous pain
God is love and God is rain
God is time and God is change

i was obsessive and immature
my heart felt ready but my mind was impure,
my soul felt connected but my mind wasn't sure
my deadly disease can't you see ?
i was the cure

—*love, rain, & change*

I thought all this time, I crossed your mind
but the only thing I crossed, was the line.
Pull me in just to push me out
how dare you say you never shared what I felt.

I can't get your name, out of my mouth
invited me in just to kick me out.
What was I supposed to think?
You say you want me then take a drink.

I don't want you
I don't need you
I don't want to need you

—my low self-esteem

Coming back to you is tiring
tried to shoot you but misfiring
is not admiring
it's madness minimizing.

Repetition and ammunition
talk so much but never listen
handles gripping
is not madness missing.

It's torturous
we always return to each other
I got you a ring
fight and cry in clustered flustered
faith as big as mustard seeds.

Reaching is a complex
tortured by my complex
of loving you like guns love hands
I am a palm
our memories are the sand
falling through the silver linings of our fingers . . .
back to you
I will always go. . .

—*my nature*

Your bones are not made of glass,
they're made of the stones you keep in your coat
the stones you'll use to skip rocks in the river
the coat that protects you from the rain
the coat that keeps you from your tears.

Your eyes are not made to cry,
they're made to describe the world to the blind
they're made to see humanity
they helped to find the man in me.

—My Amelie

Where do full moons and bright suns meet?
Is it where we make love and taboos meet?
Or by the tattoo on your feet?

Is it distant and forever gone?
Silent words always seem strong.
Gliding to horizons both pale and colorblind
look and tell me what you find.
Is it your starry thoughts or mine?
Is it finally the home you've always craved?

Blankets of clouds wrap you tight
hold you tight all through the night.
For you I'd go around the globe
if you would just wait then we'd know.
Don't let go.

It's the grey in the outcast
the silver lines on my mask
take it off and curve the crescent
last time Lord knows I learned what i lacked.

Burn the Beauty of Day
I'll Wait & Wait Always.

—for you

No matter if I leave
no matter if I stay,
i'll always be here for you
when you go away.

Go fall in love with your fantasies
while my heart continues blabbering
i will find the man in me
i'll do that just for you.

I'll always be around
even when your eyes turn
ocean blue from forest brown
i'll be the ocean and the trees.

I'll save you from yourself
when you start to drown
and be the earth
when you touch the ground.

So if you ever
follow your heart
and change your mind
i'll be who you love
each and every time.

—adaptable

Affinity,
when i seen you with your nose in a book
Infinity,
when you told me you loved me

—i remember

I found that my mind is like a garden.
She's the daisies
She's the roses
She's the lilies
She's the daffodils

They all have their own place in my garden.
But I realized,
I cannot water them the same
but I can treat all of them the same
with love & kindness

—*The Gardener*

i would flinch when he raised his hand,
the defenseless child from the angry man
my mother would flinch too
even when he didn't mean to
i never liked when he was angry
i never like when he was drunk
i remember the smell of his breath
his words mumbled his eyes sunk
like the ocean swallows sail boats in a storm
kick me yell the sting of misery
feel the burn from the tape
lock me in i crawled out
right behind you
words could not escape the mouth
kick me yell till i cry
idolize and petrified
never will i
ever know why

—*the child and the monster*

i was born to live
even though i will die
i remember as a kid
i always asked why

my father always told me
to stop asking questions
sooner or later i stopped
i receded into the confines of me
into the realm of lunacy

for i have or never will be enough
my self-worth turned selfish from insecurities
killing myself slowly from absurdities
obscurities will bury me
at this rate i will not make it past twenty-three

—I'm twenty-two

the abused becomes the abuser
the used becomes the user
the controlled becomes the tyrant
the innocent become the violent

—a half-truth

do you find love
or
does love find you ?

—ambiguity

Show me how to fake a smile
everyone sees right through me
my heart is on my sleeve
anxiety makes it hard to breathe.
How do you do it ?

—The girl that always smiles

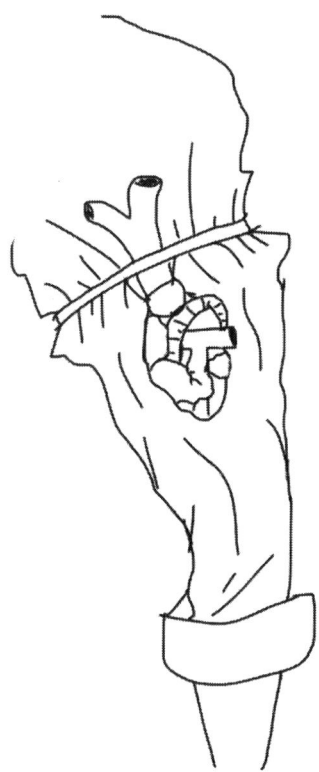

We can make love
and show our scars,
trade our pain
and let down our guard.

I can be who you want
you can be whoever you are
passion or solely flesh
it's your choice.

We can bite lips
or not kiss at all
be icy as the winter
or fluorescent as the fall.

—seasonal love

coffee stains on poetry pages
sugar sweet how lovely this stage is
close the book keep the rage in
wake up from, cries of ravens

spill the poison, on your nightstand
drink it down till you drown
chemical unbalance,
from drinking poison by the gallons
feel the slits
from raven talons

cry stagnant rivers
upon your sheets
stained with blood
that is sweet
cherry wine turned smokey & bitter
rust you must
you were born to wither

—fate

i am no dreamer
a realist at most
a cynic at least
and an arrogant fool all at once

—the angel & the arrogant

How did depression & heartbreak become romanticized ?
How did I become infatuated with Death ?
How did I become what I hate
in a matter of a breath ?

—toxic air

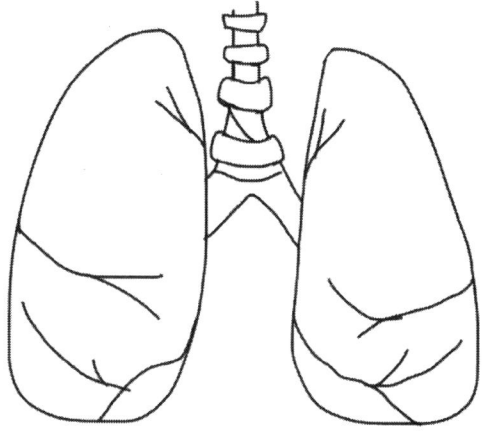

The world's afflictions
weigh heavy on my heart,
the chaos & destruction
is tearing me apart.

There is no peace
when there are no pieces to share,
we fight over religion
or even what we wear.

I find no solace
in this place of material,
based on status
I am ethereal.

I only find hope
with a child's laugh,
human kindness
when no one needs ask.

There seems few joys
many ill-stricken roads,
bad seeds come plenty
am I reaping what I sowed ?

—*threads*

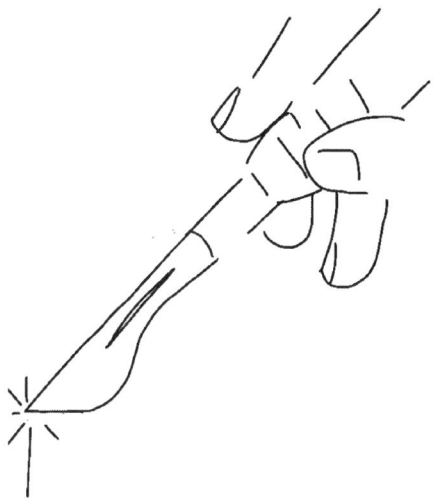

A heart of atrophy
a mind of catastrophe,
look me in my eyes
and dissect my
anatomy.

—*hello stranger*

I remember you'd sleep for days.
I heard your cries and your mumbled praise.
You told me T*he Lord is the truth,*
so explain why *The Lord* touched you ?

Every day you didn't want to wake,
how did you make it this far?
Did it help I brought you coffee
and spilled it in our hallways ?
Did me not being there help ?
Did you hate yourself?

Pain is truth or so I heard,
you told me you wish you were a bird.
What did you see
had to be done ?
I'm sorry for you pain

—y*our only son*

i was on the verge
of kissing death
she arose and was not a rose
she spoke with sweet words with an icy breath
she wanted me to rest on thorns as her welcomed guest

i was depressed
i was isolated from love and life
she wanted to be with me
i wanted her as my wife

i said
till death make us whole
and life bring us grief
my fate i have sown
my life you can keep

but then i awoke to the loudest silence my soul had ever heard
i looked out my window and found the crow on the roof,

The Blackbird.

i was disgusted at what i did
it was difficult to look myself in the mirror the next day
i just met her that night and our bodies danced
but i didn't like the dance
we stepped on each others feet
more like stomped
it was terrible
she scratched, wanted me to choke,
her moan didn't excite me
she wasn't you
she was an imposter
she finished
she left
i laid empty and alone

—one night stand

Before I wake, will you take
your pale hands to open up the blinds ?

Before I wake, can I dream ?
I'm sailing away, far away
flames of sun rays
burning out like ashtrays

Since I can't sleep anymore
will you open up the front and back door?
Let the wind in and day breath
sky blue with a May's heat
fall colors and a rain street

Before I sleep, can I walk ?
to the green flower field
where creation stays still

Before I sleep, can I weep?
'Cause I can't dream anymore
as harsh as the rain pours
insomnia closes dreamer doors

Since I can't dream anymore
will you close up the front and back door ?
Let the wind die and day sleep
overcast while Holocene seeps
fall colors and a rain street

—the broken home

Tears of Gold running down your face,
silver tongue that cannot taste.
Try to change it's a little too late,
all your life has went to waste.

Tears of Gold from the Soul that you've sold
silver lining in the clouds that stay cold.
Try to change but your fate's set in stone
black thumb deep in your bones.

Luck is for the unfortunate.
Chance is desperation.
Truth is for the righteous
and money is for segregation.

Tears of Gold running down your face,
silver tongue that cannot taste.
Try to change it's a little too late,
all your life has went to waste.

—*Silver Tongue*

My body is plagued
My vision blurred
I tried to talk but my words slurred

I'm the cure
she cried to me
I turn around and she mirrors me

I see a woman
with tears in her eyes
her sockets as bright as the sunrise

I'm on a boat
in the sea
there is nothing but water surrounding me

I see her there
with long black hair
I feel fear but then rage
she is the chapter you read silently, the ripped out pages

She is my temptress
waiting for my sympathy
now we're strangers, a ballad of sad symphonies

I look to the shadow skies
and wish for death
She haunts me with every breath

—

do you look for him in me
i asked.

does he look for me in himself
i followed.

do you sigh when he doesn't kiss you like i did
i continued.

do you wish i would tell you i'm ready for you?
you didn't reply...

i opened my eyes and realized
i was carving my notebook with a pen

—it's lonely without you

Ugliness has its beauty
while beauty has its ills
Hell is hotter than ice
in fire you get chills

Demons were once angels
the tip of the iceberg is getting warmer
Angels have broken wings
and know the true meaning of torture

God doesn't hear me but even if he did
I stopped praying when I was a kid
Tongues of distress licked the sadness
I'm a lost cause lost in madness

Innocence turns to broken purity
our light stolen our sob story
We're all guilty
We're all guilty confined in purgatory!

God doesn't hear me but even if he did
I stopped praying when I was a kid
Tongues of distress licked the sadness
I'm a lost cause lost in madness!

God doesn't hear me, he never did
He never did, he never did!
He never did . . .

—

for a long time i didn't feel free
i felt like i belonged to you
even after you cheated
even after you were with others
even after you went away to college
i always felt like i belonged to you

what kept me was the words you said
you're the only person i want to marry

all actions seemed justified in my head
the words became my chain linked to you
you knew this but did nothing
it was five years later when i let go
you told me *i let go of that idea of you and me*

and at that moment i could feel
you put the key in
the cobwebbed shackles
and open them

—*the taste of freedom*

the others are like pencils i never use
you're the pen i abuse
the others are witnesses
i am the accused.

—*reddish rues*

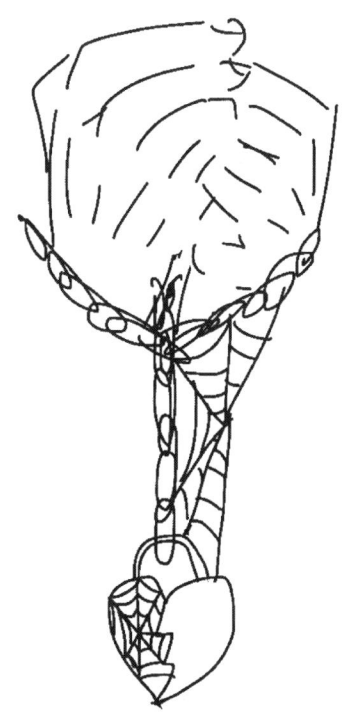

i tried to love myself how i loved others
but i lacked motivation
i didn't see the point
i was high-maintenance
i was too sensitive
i talked too much
i was awkward
i didn't talk enough
i played my music too loud
i didn't have a future to be proud of
i didn't have enough to offer
i didn't challenge myself
i didn't write enough
i wrote too much
i had ideas with no action

—self-doubt

nobody taught me how to take care of myself
i didn't know how to shave my face
i didn't wash my hair or body as often as i should have
i never washed my face
i didn't go to the doctors when i was too sick to get out of bed
i didn't sleep enough
i didn't get enough sun so i would be pale as the moonlight
but then i met you
you showed me how to be gentle with you and with myself
you showered me with love and affection when you didn't have any for yourself

—Thank you Celesté

you gave me something
nobody had ever given me
you made it from scratch
from the leather cover to the rustic pages
to the strings that had a compass attached

—the first journal i filled

I was a ghost
but then you seen me
I made the most
but then I disappeared

I thought you were the only one
you made me feel like the only one
but now I am the lonely one
but now you are the lonely one

I can't look at you the same
the mirror in the room
reflects my shame

You can't look at you the same
the fear in doom
connects the pain

You're
You're not
You're not her
You're not her anymore

You're
You're not
You're not her
And I'm not him anymore...

—strangers

scars are my tattoos

you will become who you love

or

you'll become who you hate

you'll create who you are

and

you'll radiate

the sun is making your eyes honey brown
your hair has strands of gold
the smell of fresh cut grass and sea salt
find the shades of blue sky
our bodies fit the mould

the ocean spray kisses our feet
reminiscences of cedar and tobacco
the taste of vinegar lingers upon my lips
your body lays next to mine

gravity is pressing on our bones
the earth is welcoming
there's love in our smiles
there's joy in the glossy reflections of you
it's mutual
it's comforting
it's a home being built of stone
not sand

-sand castles

her body was the canvas
my body the paintbrush
i stroked
gentle and careful
she came and i seen a canvas full of art

—my easel

her body was a meadow in spring
through all of the seasons
between her legs
lied the nectar of love
my tongue's taste buds
were the bees to and fro

—to taste you

i want to fall in love and be delusional
i don't like the real world anymore
there's no alluring illusions here only confusion
dead grass with no flowers blooming
baby booming
days are glooming
i just want life to stop but it's always moving

—*life*

i shaved my head.
i forgot that i looked like him.
i hate it just like i want to hate myself.
it's what i want.

—comfort cuts

there is no ordinance
in this place of pain
only swollen pride
like pasta never strained

—*dinner*

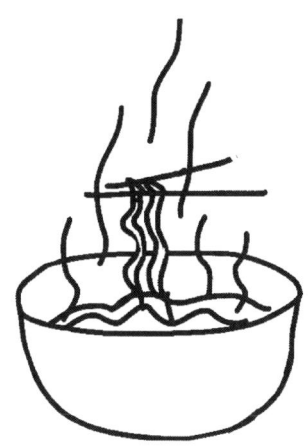

she was molested as a child

she was pressured into an abortion

she was raped

—the three women i love

i am so sorry they hurt you
i am so sorry i was one of them
i could never understand your pain.
but i can hear your story
i can listen
i can hold you
i can tell you *everything is going to be okay*
even when we both know it isn't.
i can kiss you on your forehead
caress you till you sleep
i can take you a bath when you can't get out of bed
i can cook for you
i'll run your errands
don't worry about it
let me cater to you
allow me to love you.
i don't want to be another man who forces you
to do something you don't want to do
tell me what to do and i'll do it
you want me to promise ?
i'll do that for you
i promise.
just tell me
talk to me
allow me to love you

—*guilt or love ?*

i have your heart
he has your body
i don't think you'll ever let me have both

—possession isn't love

if God is love
then God is a beautiful woman
if God is rain
then God is your stormy eyes
if God is timeless change
then God is you

—endless

I'm impatient
because i still remember the nine year old me
sitting on that small boulder outside my house
waiting for my dad to come pick me up.

It was his weekend.
He said he was on his way four hours ago i thought
My bags have been packed for five hours.
Maybe traffic?
or
He had something important to take care of?
He wouldn't forget.

It's getting dark outside.
Maybe he forgot where we live?
Maybe my mom gave him the wrong address
Where is he?

—a call came weeks later that he was in jail

The author isn't on my side in my life story
at times i feel like he or she ignores me
pours, rain on me in the sunshine
gives me sight then makes me blind
treats me cruel then very kind

i don't understand
is this a comedy or tragedy ?
is this love or catastrophe ?
are you mad at me?
are you projecting your insecurities ?
i hope you know
you're hurting me . . .

i can feel,
it's how you made me
i'm full of loving, not hating
so stop trying to change me
i'm sensitive
i've always had a heart
truth be written
i don't want your words to turn me cold & harsh

—*the writer & the protagonist*

there's religion and there's spirituality
there's only delusions with no real reality
there's logic and there's true fallacies
there's our infinite universe in an empty galaxy
so i don't believe in God
at least not the one you do
the God *you* believe in
is selfish
he claims unconditional love
with all these conditions.

—we cannot know anything for certain without faith—

you are the foundation of my heart
the keeper of my soul,
the bedrock of my passion
the warmth when i am cold.

i find stagnancy when you are away
my heart goes to atrophy when you are astray,
i need not the touch of your hands but the heart on your throat
you give me sanctuary when i have no hope.

when i am lost
i find you love me wherever i trek,
you give me more depth
more love
more connection without the single thought of sex.

if you were to leave
i would never find solace,
you are the truth you are kindness
when my lips are honest.

my days would go numb and bleak
if you were to leave this life's sight,
because this world would lose a light
that could never be replaced,
you are the companion of my soul
you are my hidden grace.

—Jessie

i am your calm serene island
and you are the storm that always comes around
you try to love me and water me
but you always flood my mounds

you shower me with love
until i cannot breathe
you shower me with care
until you want to leave

which is never
which is why i grow embers
in my volcanic eyes
while you continue to shower me
with your oblivion of non-platonic cries
it's your pride

i start to flood and mud turns to swamps
beaches turn to marshes debris start to flaunt
and that is when you go away
when i'm in ruins
and as soon as flowers bloom
you return and bring your doom

—the island

they say home is where the heart is
but i think home is where the heart breaks

—home

my favourite thing about you was
when you'd say *look up*
i'd gazed at the sky and then at you
i'd think to myself *you are a child of the moon*

when i left you
your voice stayed near
when i was walking alone
look up is what i'd hear

i'd look up and see the sky
adore it and admire it with my eyes
i'd see you staring back
with green eyes of your old black cat
if i could, i hope you know i would
take it all back

—things i never said

i don't like when you lie
because i force myself to believe you
even though to me
your deception
i always see through

your deceit and habits
are the untold fabric
of the truth i know
you're an actress

i allow you to fool me
because i am lonely
so i wonder if
i'm the hidden phony

—*you or me*

Sometimes i grow tired of being on my own
my eyes want to cry but my tears take no form,
My heart aches from being alone
the cruelty i've allowed, i'm bitter and torn.

I've craved to be noticed and truly adored
but now what occupies my mental is envy and scorn.
i smell the roses and i inhale the thorns
my heart tried to tell me
i can't say i wasn't warned.

Sometimes i grow tired of being tired
it's dreadful to feel like this
i'm tired of being tired
how aren't you tired too?

—the ills

my sister

my father

my first love

all tried to commit suicide

take care of my daughter when i'm gone
my sister said before she attempted

i love you son
were the last words i ever heard from my father

i never asked *her* what happened

—i wish i could have done more

people have always loved your smile
they always seen your light
even as a kid
everyone knew that you were bright
but you grew up around drugs
lack of love and abuse
so that smile hid under layers,
and yet you were loved abundantly
you were in other's prayers.
you were around lies and part of you died
absent of your youth
you were from a broken home
a father that beat your mother into truth.
you were broken mentally
the violence with no remedy
hurt constantly you killed enemies
human nature was commonly horrid
you may have killed to shield
your outlook turned morbid
mental torture grew
mind turned blue
rage at an age
perspective was skewed
you couldn't face it. . .
they only seen anger and the incomplacence
not when you were a kid and that man lured you to his basement. . .

—my father

who were you
before all the hurt?
were you the only flower in the garden
with roots in the earth?
were you pure
even though you grew in the dirt?
or were you shy and meek
because you didn't know of your worth?
were you fluorescent and free
with scents heavenly?
were you free to choose your life
or are things meant to be?
did people wanting to possess you
affect you growth?
did you feeling guilty
make you sacrifice your hopes?
did you running away
teach you how to cope?
did you having nothing
help you make the most,
of a life full of struggle
in a world full of don'ts?
who were you?

—*to my mother*

your heart will break
if you try to love her
you'll try to be different
but you're only another

you'll feel unwanted
and empty with envy
your love will turn obsessive
you'll dissect every memory

you'll forget your friends
you won't know self-care
you'll be so focused on her
you won't know what's out there

time will pass
and things will change
you won't let go
so you'll feel the angst

but sooner or later

you will move on
and you'll truly think it'll last
but you're addicted to *her*
you will inevitably relapse

—*cycles*

there is a time and place
to fill empty space
when i'm ready
i will feel

but i know it won't be the same
because you are not you
you are the polaroid picture
i took of you

somewhere you gave up
and in that place you died
i see it in your actions
i see it in your abyss
of brown eyes

maybe it was the bottles
with the strange names
the numb nulling nature
of pain

or the inability to
maintain your chaos
the triggered traumas you cannot escape
the cancer of change.

—change stays the same

our love was strong
our love was true,
there was even a time
i needed you.

i've been depressed
i've been in the midst of euphoria,
i even thought
we could build a utopia.

but foolish young romance
mixed with emotional desperate attempts,
made every meaningful thing i did
meaningless and exempt.

—*foreverless*

i remember the first day i seen you
you were the girl from my dreams
a spitting image
i couldn't believe my eyes
you were an idea put into existence

but little did i know
it didn't matter my persistence
we would never be
i could only love you from afar
like a telescope loves the stars
it didn't matter
my dark matter

little did i know
i'd watch you travel
i'd watch you grow and unravel
your soul's akathreads
delicately and sometime too rough

little did you know
you'd lose the battle
because when you want peace
you co-create war
so beliefs are nothing but
a house with no doors

—*across the room*

my heart dropped when you told me.
i think it may have fell through my stomach
and tumbled to the floor by my seat,
or maybe it flew out
the window of the car
and was run over in the street ?
or maybe it fell by the gas pedal
and it was hammered by your feet ?

my eyes want to create saltwater
that would pump from my heartbeat,
maybe the liquid would leak
from the holes in my heart
and the holes in my feet
my heart wants to rot and shriek
because times are bleak, my heart is stale
there is no hope this is no fairytale

because a part of me died
when you told me of this fate,
if i said *i wish that it was me*
it would have been too late.

so the heart-aching truth is
i will never end up with you,
this is the end of our possibility
the finality of you.

—*a baby in your belly*

you will take what happened to the tomb
you carry a life in your womb
and death in your mind
there's pressure from *him*
will you give in?

there's pressure from him again
there's pressure now within
pressure from your mother
pressure found its way in
you're thinking it over
your thoughts are tainted with his ego,
not with your love for this creation
the pain was sharp as a needle
in your uterus
you still remember,
you'll always remember

you'll start to imagine if the baby would have been a boy or girl
you'll fill their pure essence in the emptiness of your mind
your tears will water the future they will never have
you'll blame yourself like you always do
you'll know full emptiness.
he doesn't care about you
stop trying to think he does.
you care more about you
and you hate yourself

—a diamond taken from your belly

What if you don't hate yourself?
What if you love yourself
and the hate is for who you've become?

Do you care as a product of your guilt
or as a product of your internal wreckage?
Do the things you never tell anyone
force you to be reckless?

Did telling everyone your issues
only result in turmoil?
Is that the reason you mix love and fear
like water and oil?

Could you ever even fully trust someone
like you did as a child?
Will the self-hate ever dissipate
and stop being so vile?

Will you ever be more than okay,
will the pills help your psyche?
Will suicide ever be something
that is unlikely for you?

—*questions i could never ask*

love may be found in the forms your tongue makes
the shapes of your mouth
and your body's torso vibrations
but it speaks every language
not just yours
it originates from a vulnerable location.
more words does not mean more love
more hands does not mean more love
silence is not anguish
it is the bridge
to speak a language of an idea
it allows you to express
exactly what and how you feel
emotions are relative
while love is an absolute.

—the universe left us love

i see sunburn speckles
your nose crinkles when you laugh
i love your freckles
i remove my mask

you tug your ears
when you're nervous
your gentle embrace
is delicate

you move your hair from your face
our irises glaze over to reflect each other
intimacy in its intricacies
i'm nervous too

we move our tongues with purpose
our bodies becoming one
your body and eyes
in the tears of the sun

we find comfort
while connection moans through drywall
our bodies sweat in sweet love
i wonder will i fall, for you
someone new

—the hopeful romantic

i want to notice every detail about you.
i want to count every freckle on your face.
i want to know the depth of the dimple on your lower back.
i want to know the shade of brown your eyes are.
i want to know what the tempo of your heart is before you sleep.

i want to know why your favorite color is every shade of blue.
i want to know why you love the sound of rain pattering on a window while you read and drink green tea.
i want to know who hurt you and learn where you got every scar.
i want to make a map of your body
and travel wherever you allow me.

i want to learn how you broke your ankle and who broke your heart.
i want to know your favorite memories that you think of when you're sad.
i want to know what you do when you're all alone.
i want to know your favorite songs and i want to know what makes you cry.
What makes you yell?
What makes you feel small?
i want to know why you don't like to be flattered but you don't mind compliments.
i want to know why you know so much but say you know nothing.

but most of all, i want to know why i want to know these things.

—i'm falling for you

i have physically lived
and anatomically died
this has happened to me
a multitude of times

my mind has been an old man
on his death bed
my mind has been a newborn
with his whole life ahead

i have witnessed different perspectives
and lived protected within my beliefs
and those same beliefs
have also shattered under my feet

i have fallen
for lies and for love
some screws have been loosened
i have lost a few lugs

i have questioned my significance
i have questioned my morals
i have expanded my mental universe
and interconnected to new portals

i am the epitome of nothing
i am the child of the universal wind
if you ask me *where are you going ?*
i'll tell you where i've been

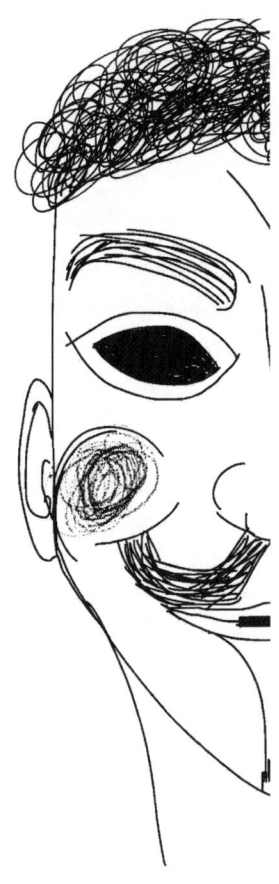

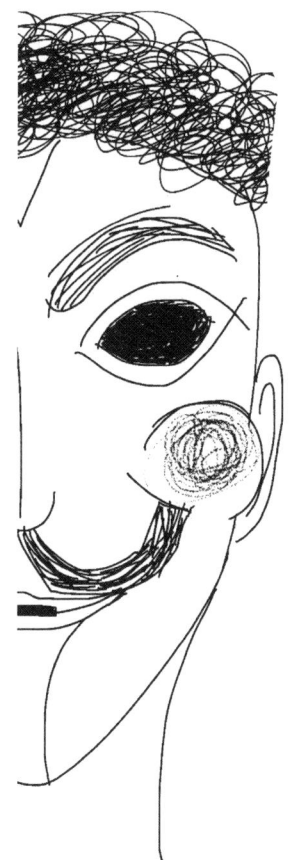

i've worn many masks
been an imposter in my flesh
i've been an outcast an outsider
and acted like the rest

i've told my story
loud and with courage
i've went with the flow
and fought with the current

i've been a friend to the lonely
a friend to myself
i've abandoned my family
when they needed help

i've loved with my entire soul
i've hated another with boiling rage
i've felt bliss without ignorance
i've wrote it all down
and ripped up the page

i've lived and i've lied
i've grown and understood
that life isn't all bad
and it isn't all good

—youniverse

i hope you know
i couldn't have done it without you
thank you for your hurt
thank you for your love
thank you for my worth

—*everything i am*

i want to thank you for reading this book. i am grateful that you took one of the most valuable things that we have as people, *time*, and gave some of it to me.

thank you, you made it through. i hope you share me with loved ones and friends or revisit me when you have some spare time or maybe hold me when you want a companion. i'll be always be here for you, frozen in time, be it laying on your nightstand, crammed in the bottom of the pouch behind the front seat of your car, between the cushions of the cafe's comfortable couch, the dusty book shelf, wherever you want me to be, i'll be there

with youniversal love

—*GARSEA*

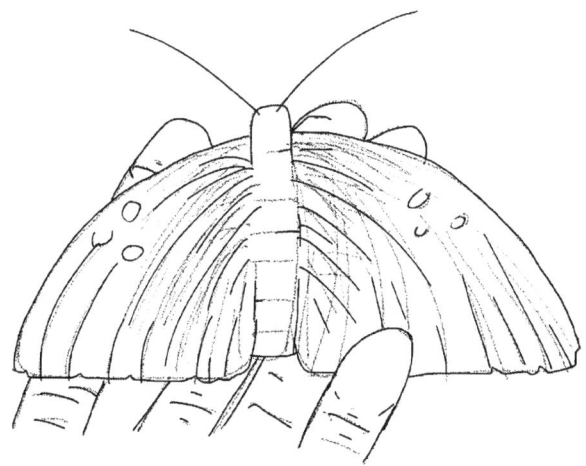

Thank you to:

My mom for never giving up on me
My dad for doing what he could, may he rest in peace
Mi Pa Fidel Orozco for showing me what a home is
Jessie for simply being.

Erica for being a friend when i had no one
Celeste for showing me how to take care of myself
My older sister Cassandra for always making sure i'm okay
Tim for always supporting and encouraging my art

Thank you to all my other friends and family!
I would not be here without you.

Special thanks to my high school English teacher
Monique Coughran who was the first person that
encouraged me to write.

and last but not least

Thank YOU for reading

Made in the USA
San Bernardino, CA
26 May 2018